Mary Anning
Fossil Hunter

Written by Anna Claybourne
Illustrated by Laura Tolton

Contents

Collins

The ichthyosaur

It's the year 1811, in Lyme Regis on Britain's south coast. A dark-haired 12-year-old girl is scrambling about on the steep, crumbling cliffs. She searches, stops, and searches again, pulling at the rocks. Then, around nine metres up the sloping cliff face, she finds what she's looking for – the fossil bones of a huge, ancient reptile.

The girl is Mary Anning, one of the greatest fossil hunters in history. Her find, an ichthyosaur fossil, is the first of her many great discoveries.

the cliffs where Mary Anning hunted for fossils

Fossil Fact

What are fossils?
Fossils are the remains or **imprints** of ancient living things, preserved in rock. They form when a plant or animal is buried and rots away, and parts of it are gradually replaced by **minerals**.

2

Months earlier, Mary's older brother Joseph had discovered a large, crocodile-like fossil head. Mary took up the search for the rest of the creature. When she found it, she asked the locals to help her dig it out. They unearthed an amazing, complete fossil skeleton. It was to inspire scientists in the new field of palaeontology – the study of **prehistoric** living things from their fossils.

This is an example of an ichthyosaur fossil.

Bright spark

Mary Anning was born in 1799, into a poor family. Her father, Richard Anning, was a carpenter. Her mother, also called Mary, was known as Molly. Richard and Molly had ten children, but only two – Mary and her older brother Joseph – survived childhood. In those days, young children often died of common illnesses, such as measles and flu.

Mary Anning's house and shop in Lyme Regis, drawn in 1842

The Anning family were Dissenters, meaning they refused to join the traditional Church of England. The Dissenters of Lyme Regis had their own church, the independent chapel. People often disapproved of Richard Anning for working on Sundays, but he was a loving father to Mary and Joseph.

As a baby, Mary cried and coughed constantly, and her parents feared she wouldn't live long. But when she was 15 months old, a strange, tragic event seemed to change her.

Molly's friend, Elizabeth Haskings, offered to take baby Mary out for the day. Elizabeth was standing under a tree with Mary and two friends, when a sudden storm broke. Lightning struck the tree, and all three women were killed. But little Mary, still in Elizabeth's arms, was alive. From that day on, everyone noticed that she was far more healthy, clever and alert than ever before.

Life in Lyme Regis

Lyme Regis, the Annings' town, is on the coast of Dorset, in southern England. For centuries, it was a major port and shipbuilding town. It's famous for its long, curving harbour wall, known as the Cobb, built from wood and stone.

The town is also known for its seaside cliffs, which are amazingly rich in fossils. They lie east of the town, towards the village of Charmouth. In fact, Lyme Regis is in the middle of a stretch of coast known as the **Jurassic** Coast, thanks to its many ancient fossils.

the Jurassic coast near Mary's home

The Cobb dates from the 1300s, but has been rebuilt several times.

In the early 1800s, many people in England were poor. Britain had been at war with France for years. This reduced **trade**, and made food very expensive. Homes had no electricity in those days, and there was little medical care. People often died young of everyday illnesses. The average life expectancy for a person born in England in 1799, like Mary Anning, was only about 40 years.

Most children didn't go to school either. But Mary did learn to read and write at Sunday school, at her parents' church.

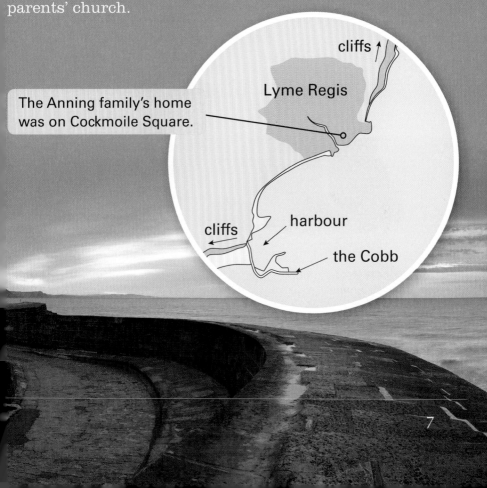

The Anning family's home was on Cockmoile Square.

cliffs

Lyme Regis

cliffs

harbour

the Cobb

The fossil stall

Mary's father struggled to make a living as a carpenter.
To bring in extra money, he collected fossils from
the beach and cliffs. He set up a stall outside the family
home, where he sold the fossils he'd found to passers-by.

Mary later said that her mother didn't like her
father's hobby. She was especially annoyed when
Richard took Joseph and Mary fossil hunting with him.
But they loved it, and Mary became very good at
spotting fossils.

Layers of rock

In prehistoric times, the area around Lyme Regis was underwater. The rocks there formed from layers of mud and minerals collecting on the sea bed. This meant the fossils found in them are mostly sea creatures. The layers of hard **limestone** and softer **shale** rock make the cliffs unstable and crumbly, so fossil collecting there can be quite dangerous.

a fish fossil found near Lyme Regis

Tourists often came to Lyme Regis to visit the seaside, and bought the curious stone shapes as **souvenirs**. However, people didn't really understand what they were, or know much about the prehistoric creatures that had formed them. They gave fossils magical, mysterious names.

Bullet-shaped **belemnites** were called "devil's fingers".

Snail-like ammonites were known as "snake-stones".

The breadwinner

In 1810, when Mary Anning was 11, disaster struck. Her father had been suffering from tuberculosis (TB), a serious lung disease, for years. He became more and more unwell after injuring himself falling on the cliffs. Finally he died, aged 44.

Now, besides their grief, the Annings were plunged into even worse poverty. Molly had to plead for "parish relief", a charity payment for the poorest families. The money was three shillings a week – about £40 today. It was barely enough to live on. A local landowner's wife, Mrs Stock, saw how clever and determined Mary was. She did her best to help the Annings by paying Mary to do **errands**. She also gave her a book about **geology**.

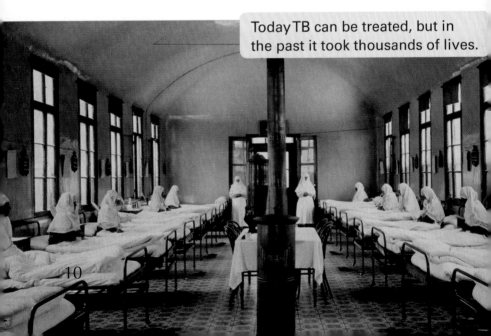

Today TB can be treated, but in the past it took thousands of lives.

One day, Mary went fossil hunting alone and found a beautiful ammonite. On her way home, a woman walking on the beach stopped her, and offered her half a crown for the fossil. That was two and a half shillings – almost a week's charity money. Mary realised that she could make a living this way, even without her father.

Ammonites are **extinct** now, but were once common sea creatures. They were similar to octopuses, but had a coiled shell.

Along with her brother Joseph, Mary Anning
returned to the beach regularly to search for fossils.
Just as their father had, they sold them on the stall
outside their house. It wasn't a very reliable income,
but it made a big difference, and helped the family
to survive.

The stonecutters

Besides fossils, Lyme Regis's cliffs were full of useful limestone. Stonecutters extracted slabs of the stone to be taken to the harbour and shipped off to London to be used for building.

holes made in the rock by stonecutters

As the workers removed large slabs of stone, they opened up gaps in the cliffs. This revealed new fossils. Mary and her brother made friends with the stonecutters, and made a deal with them. If the stonecutters spotted anything exciting in the rock, they would call the Annings to come and see it. In return, the stonecutters would be paid a small fee for helping to dig out the fossils.

Fossil fact

Rock science
Before Mary Anning's time, people had little idea about how rocks and fossils formed. The science of geology was only just getting started. But during the early 1800s, it was to become an important part of science – partly thanks to Mary Anning's work.

The stone crocodile

The year after her father died, 12-year-old Mary discovered her famous ichthyosaur. Joseph found its fossilised head in the spring, close to the village of Charmouth, and thought it was a crocodile. Joseph had started an **apprenticeship** as an **upholsterer**, so he was too busy to look for the rest. He asked Mary to find it if she could.

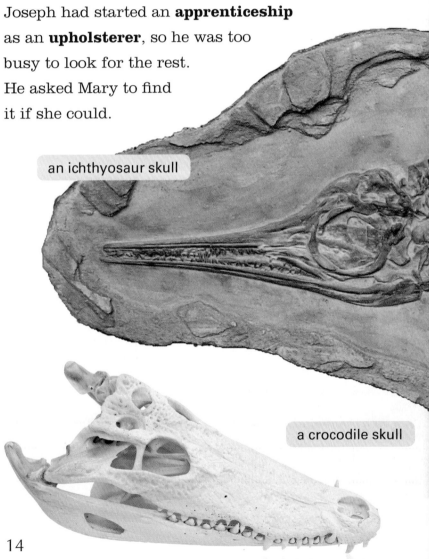

an ichthyosaur skull

a crocodile skull

At first, Mary had no luck. But after a winter storm damaged the cliffs, she found several large vertebrae, or backbones. The stonecutters helped her dig out more and more of the skeleton. Meanwhile, word spread that Mary had found an amazing creature in the cliffs.

Over several months, Mary collected almost all the bones of an enormous creature. It was around 5 metres long – the size of a great white shark. And one thing was clear. It didn't look much like a crocodile.

Fossil Fact Q

What's an ichthyosaur?

An ichthyosaur (pronounced "*ikth*-ee-uh-sor") is a type of prehistoric sea creature. Like dinosaurs, ichthyosaurs were reptiles. The name ichthyosaur means "fish-lizard", and ichthyosaurs looked similar to today's dolphins and sharks. They lived from around 250 to 90 million years ago, and ranged from 1 metre to a whopping 16 metres long – bigger than a bus.

Mary's skills

All this time, Mary was getting better and better at finding fossils. But that wasn't her only skill. She also knew how to break apart the stone around each fossil with her hammer, gently so as not to damage it. Mary then prepared and cleaned the fossils, to show their details clearly, and often drew sketches of her discoveries as well.

If a fossil had many separate parts, Mary had to fit them together to show what the whole animal looked like. For this, she had to understand animal skeletons, joints, teeth and other parts. Years of experience comparing and identifying fossils made her an expert on prehistoric sea creatures.

ammonite

starfish

belemnite

fish

crinoid

shark tooth

some of the types of fossils found at Lyme Regis

Fossil Fact Q

Jigsaw puzzles

In the early days of palaeontology, scientists often weren't sure how to fit skeletons together. One famous example was the dinosaur *iguanodon*. It was discovered by early palaeontologist Gideon Mantell in the 1820s. Mantell found a strange spike among the bones, so he put it on the dinosaur's nose. Later, other scientists found that *iguanodon* actually had two spikes, which were on its thumbs.

Sold!

After cleaning and preparing the huge fossil creature they'd found, the Annings put it up for sale. Local landowner Henry Hoste Henley bought it for £23 – that's about £1,700 today. It was enough money to support Mary's family for half a year.

Henley sold the fossil on again, to a museum owner, William Bullock. He displayed it in his Museum of Natural **Curiosities** in London. Many scientists came to see it, and it sparked a huge **debate**.

The scientist Sir Everard Home studied the fossil, and declared it was definitely not a crocodile. It was then sold again – for an even higher price of £48 – to the British Museum. There, curator Charles Koenig came up with the name ichthyosaur, or "fish-lizard".

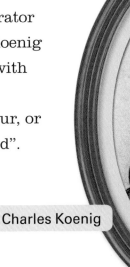

Charles Koenig

18

In the 19th century, many people believed religious teachings that the earth was only a few thousand years old, and that all living things had been created just as they are now. But fossils like this showed that different creatures had once lived on Earth. This raised questions about whether animals had actually changed, or evolved, over time.

However, no one thought to ask Mary's opinion, or to credit her and Joseph with discovering the fossil.

Bullock's Museum of Natural Curiosities

The fossil expert

While scientists were arguing over her ichthyosaur,
Mary Anning grew up. Joseph had finished his
apprenticeship and become an upholsterer, and Mary
took over the family fossil business, along with
her mother. Besides collecting and selling fossils, Mary
began to make friends in the world of science.

One friend was Henry De la Beche, a local boy
who'd studied geology. There was also William
Buckland, an **eccentric**, fossil-obsessed **clergyman**.
In 1818, he became the first professor of Geology at
Oxford University. Friends like these would visit Mary
to buy fossils, or go fossil collecting with her. In return,
she borrowed books and papers from them, learning
about the latest ideas in palaeontology.

Another friend was a wealthy local fossil collector,
Thomas Birch. He liked Mary's family, and was upset
to see that despite Mary's hard work, they were still
desperately poor. So Birch organised a sale of fossils
he'd bought from them in the past, which was held
in London. Well-known scientists flocked to buy
them, and Birch gave the money to the Annings.
Through the sale, many more geologists heard about
Mary Anning.

Who's who?

Henry De la Beche

Henry De la Beche was born into a wealthy family. When he was young, his father died, and he and his mother moved to Lyme Regis, where he made friends with Mary Anning. He became one of Britain's leading geologists. In 1835, he started the British Geological Survey, an organisation that studies and maps the geology of Britain. It still exists today.

A new creature

After finding her first ichthyosaur, Mary discovered several more. They were different from each other, revealing that there must have been many ichthyosaur **species**. Then, in the winter of 1820–21, Mary found something different. Like the ichthyosaur, it seemed to be a sea reptile. However, it was a different shape, with a very long neck. The head was missing, but in 1823, Mary found another, complete **specimen**. Its head was smaller and shorter than an ichthyosaur's head, giving the creature a snake-like look.

The plesiosaur

The new animal caused a sensation amongst scientists, who rushed to study it. Henry De la Beche and another geologist, William Conybeare, named it the plesiosaur, or "near-lizard".

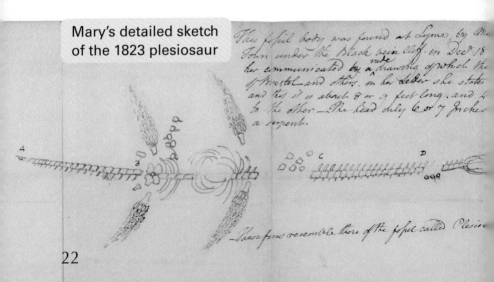

Mary's detailed sketch of the 1823 plesiosaur

However, the famous French naturalist George Cuvier declared that the creature was so strange, it must be a **hoax**. The Geological Society of London, a club for geologists, held a special meeting about it. Luckily, they decided the fossil was **genuine**, saving Mary Anning's reputation.

In 1824, William Conybeare made a presentation about the plesiosaur to the Geological Society. He used sketches by Mary Anning as part of it. Yet, like others before him, he didn't credit her for her work.

Plesiosaurs were fish-eating sea reptiles.

Anning's Fossil Depot

In 1826, using money she'd made from her finds, Mary Anning opened her own fossil shop. It was on Broad Street in the middle of Lyme Regis, and was named Anning's Fossil Depot.

a later photo of Mary Anning's fossil shop in Lyme Regis

Mary, Joseph and their mother left their old house and moved in above the shop. It was a step up for them, to a nicer part of town, and a more respected place in Lyme Regis society.

Anning's Fossil Depot became a magnet for fossil-lovers from all over the world. As well as tourists and collectors, many scientists came to see it. They wanted to talk to Mary herself about her fossils. They often then used the things she'd told them in their own work.

Though she was often not given credit for her ideas, Mary was becoming increasingly well-known as a fossil finder. A London magazine described her as "the well-known fossilist, whose labours lately have **enriched** the British Museum".

Geologist George William Featherstonhaugh travelled all the way from America to visit Anning's Fossil Depot. He bought a selection of fossils for a new museum in New York.

Fossil ink

Among the most common types of fossils at Lyme Regis are belemnites. When these extinct animals were alive, they looked similar to a squid. But unlike a modern squid, they had a hard, pointed skeleton at one end, shaped like a bullet.

belemnites

One day, Mary cut open a belemnite fossil and noticed something inside it. It was a tiny **sac**, containing what looked like old dried-up ink. She showed it to her friend Elizabeth Philpot, who was an artist as well as a fossil-lover. Elizabeth mixed the powder with water and made a brownish ink, just like the **sepia** made from the ink of modern **cuttlefish**.

belemnite fossils

Squid squirt ink at enemies to confuse them, while they escape.

Mary showed belemnites containing ink to her friend William Buckland. He used them to write a paper showing that prehistoric belemnites had used ink as a defence, just as today's squid, octopuses and cuttlefish do.

Elizabeth Philpot was 20 years older than Mary Anning, but they were close friends, and often went fossil hunting together. Elizabeth had a brilliant fossil collection, and was an expert on fossil fish. She was also an artist and painted detailed pictures of fossils.

Elizabeth Philpot's painting of an ichthyosaur fossil

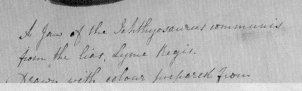

A jaw of the Ichthyosaurus communis from the lias, Lyme Regis. Drawn with colour prepared from

27

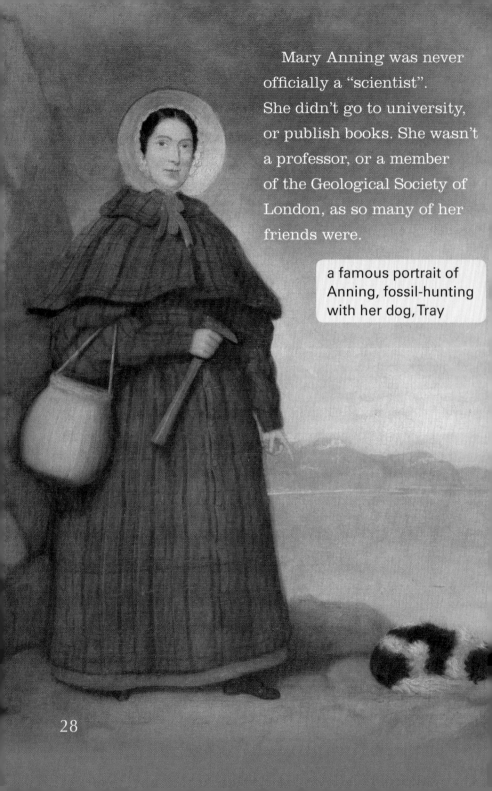

Mary Anning was never officially a "scientist". She didn't go to university, or publish books. She wasn't a professor, or a member of the Geological Society of London, as so many of her friends were.

a famous portrait of Anning, fossil-hunting with her dog, Tray

However, in terms of what she knew about fossils and prehistoric life, Mary was one of the world's leading palaeontologists. She didn't just discover fossils; she also identified them, studied them and came up with ideas about how prehistoric creatures had lived. She read all the geology books and **scientific papers** she could, and although she couldn't go to scientific meetings in London, she knew what went on there. Her scientist friends, such as William Buckland and Henry De la Beche, always wrote to her and kept her updated.

When Mary made discoveries, it was often William Buckland who wrote them up and presented them to other scientists. William had started out as a clergyman, but eventually became a leading geologist and palaeontologist. He was known for his endless curiosity and enthusiasm, and was one of Mary's closest friends.

William Buckland was an expert on dinosaurs, and studied megalosaurs, one of the first dinosaurs known.

William Buckland

Left out

Why couldn't Mary Anning take her rightful place at the centre of British science? There were several reasons. Firstly, as a poor, working-class person, she couldn't afford to study at university, or even at a normal school. This meant she couldn't get an official scientific job. Secondly, Mary came from a family of Dissenters. Dissenters couldn't go to university or have certain jobs, such as being a teacher.

The main reason, however, was that Mary was a woman. In her time, just 200 years ago, women couldn't study at university, or join science clubs like the Geological Society of London. They were a man's world.

The Geological Society of London finally allowed women to join in 1919.

Of course, many women worked – just not in well-paid, "professional" jobs. And there were plenty of female fossil experts, like Mary's friend Elizabeth Philpot. Some male geologists, including William Buckland, had wives who worked with them. They collected fossils, drew sketches and had ideas. It was just that the men took most of the credit.

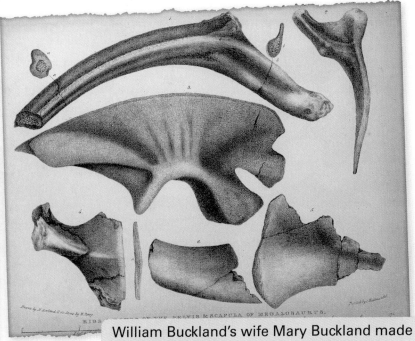

William Buckland's wife Mary Buckland made these drawings for a paper he published.

As Mary Anning never got married, she couldn't even work in that way. Instead, she relied on friends like William Buckland to present her discoveries and theories.

Credit at last

In December 1828, after a spell of finding very few fossils, 29-year-old Mary Anning made a fabulous new discovery. It was a "winged-lizard", or pterosaur. This was a flying or gliding reptile, related to dinosaurs.

The fossil was jumbled up, but Mary recognised the parts that showed it had wings and a long tail.

Fossilised bones of pterosaurs had been found before, in Germany, but Anning's fossil was almost complete. It was the first pterosaur ever found in Britain.

Not surprisingly, the remains of pterosaurs reminded people of dragons. In fact, pterosaur bones dug up in ancient times might explain where myths about dragons came from.

As usual, Mary's friend William Buckland announced the find. He studied the fossil carefully, and prepared a paper describing the creature. In February 1829, he presented it to the Geological Society of London. This time, he took care to mention that it was Mary Anning who'd found it.

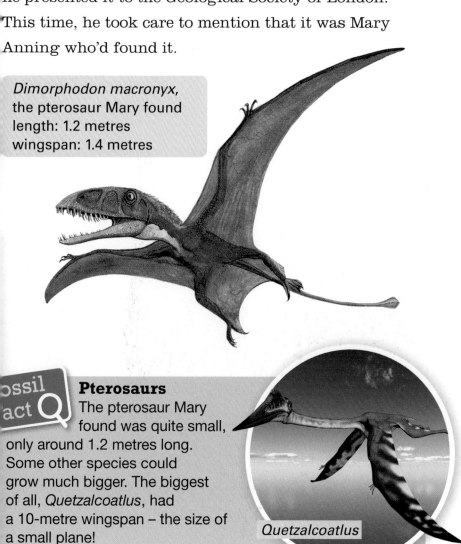

Dimorphodon macronyx, the pterosaur Mary found
length: 1.2 metres
wingspan: 1.4 metres

Fossil fact

Pterosaurs
The pterosaur Mary found was quite small, only around 1.2 metres long. Some other species could grow much bigger. The biggest of all, *Quetzalcoatlus*, had a 10-metre wingspan – the size of a small plane!

Quetzalcoatlus

Everyday fossils

Today, Mary Anning is best-known for her exciting large finds. However, these were few and far between. Working hard at the cliffs every day, she mainly unearthed smaller fossils such as belemnites, ammonites and fish. These kept her business going, and taught her more and more about the different families and species of prehistoric life.

an example of a fish fossil Mary found at Lyme Regis, known as *Dapedium politum*

Mary Anning also spent a lot of time reading, sketching, and meeting up with her scientist friends. She worked for many hours in her shop too. Children especially loved going there. Just like children today, they were fascinated by the beautiful ammonites and fossil shells on display.

Mary was always kind and patient with them. In the late 1800s, a woman named Nellie Waring wrote about visiting Anning's Fossil Depot as a child. She said:

> "Our pocket-money was freely spent on the little ammonites which she washed and **burnished** till they shone like metal ... She would see to us with the sweetest temper, never finding us too troublesome as we turned over her trays of curiosities."

A modern-day fossil shop in Lyme Regis, where fossils are still a popular souvenir.

Fossil poos

Cone-shaped fossils known as "bezoar stones" or "fossil fir cones" were common in Lyme Regis.

bezoar stones

Some people believed they had magical healing powers.

Mary Anning noticed that she often found these fossils among ichthyosaur bones. She also discovered that they had small bones inside them. She realised that they must be the fossilised poos of ichthyosaurs and other sea creatures. She shared her ideas with William Buckland, and they worked together on the discovery. Buckland gave fossil poos their scientific name, "coprolites".

Studying coprolites could reveal what prehistoric creatures ate. They're still an important part of palaeontology to this day.

This dinosaur poo is 140 million years old.

The big city

In 1829, when Mary Anning was 30, she left the Lyme Regis area for the only time in her life, for a trip to London. She visited the British Museum and the Geological Society of London, where her finds were often presented and displayed.

In London, Mary stayed with her friends Charlotte and Roderick Murchison. Charlotte was a passionate palaeontologist. As she couldn't be a professional geologist herself, she'd encouraged her husband to become one instead, so that she could work with him. She was one of Mary's closest friends.

Roderick Murchsion giving a lecture

Hard times

In 1830, poverty struck again. Mary, now aged 31, hadn't made any big finds for some time, and her money was running out. Her old friend, the geologist Henry De la Beche, came up with an idea to help her. He painted a scene of prehistoric life in Dorset, based on Mary's fossil finds. Then he had it made into a print, and sold copies to all his friends. He gave all the **proceeds** to Mary.

Henry De la Beche's picture was called *Duria Antiquior – a more ancient Dorset*. It included plesiosaurs, ichthyosaurs, pterosaurs and other sea creatures.

Today, we're used to realistic images of ancient creatures. They began thanks to Mary Anning's fossils.

Scientists loved the print, and used it to help teach their students. It was the first ever picture of life in prehistoric times, based on real fossils.

Henry De la Beche also often drew cartoons about prehistoric creatures, like this one.

By now, Mary's brother Joseph had met and married his wife, Amelia, and moved out of the Anning family home. He and Amelia went on to have six children, although three of them died young. Joseph continued to help Mary and Molly with their business, but had to spend most of his time on his own work and family.

Another breakthrough

In December 1830, Mary struck gold again. Winter was always a good time for fossil finds, as the winter wind and waves broke chunks off the cliffs. Mary discovered another, almost perfect, plesiosaur fossil. It was missing just one flipper and part of its tail. It was curled up in an amazingly clear position, and had a very large head.

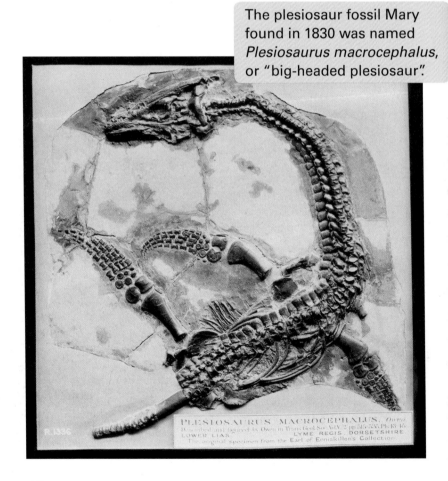

The plesiosaur fossil Mary found in 1830 was named *Plesiosaurus macrocephalus*, or "big-headed plesiosaur".

Mary excitedly wrote to tell William Buckland the news. She said: "It is without exception the most beautiful fossil I have ever seen." The fossil was soon sold to a collector, and the dinosaur expert Richard Owen studied it and wrote a paper about it. To Mary's annoyance, he didn't mention her.

A change of church

Mary had always attended the independent chapel for Dissenters in Lyme Regis. But around this time, she switched churches, joining the traditional Anglican church. This might have been because the old pastor John Gleed, a fossil-lover, left the Dissenter chapel, and she didn't like the new pastor. Many of her friends, such as William Buckland, were Anglicans too. Mary remained very religious all her life.

St Michael's Anglican church in Lyme Regis has a window dedicated to Mary Anning.

Avalanche

For many years, Mary had owned a black-and-white terrier, Tray. He was her **adored companion**, and went with her on fossil-collecting trips. She'd trained him to stand guard over fossils when she had to go for help to dig them out. When she returned, thanks to Tray, she could easily find the right spot again.

a sketch by Mary Anning of her dog, Tray

One day in October 1833, Mary was on the beach with Tray when she heard a loud cracking and rumbling noise. It was the sound of a mass of loose stone falling from the crumbling cliffs. There was no time to get out of the way. Before her eyes, an avalanche of rock and mud rushed down the slope and swallowed the dog up. There was no chance of him surviving.

Mary was devastated. Rock falls were a risk for anyone collecting fossils at Lyme Regis. The best fossils were found after storms, when the rocks were often loose, and could fall without warning. Mary had been lucky so far, but losing her beloved Tray made her worried. She knew she'd been inches away from losing her own life too.

There are often rock falls at Lyme Regis today.

A name in science

By now, Mary Anning was very famous, and leading geologists often came to ask her advice. One of these was a well-known Swiss-born palaeontologist, Louis Agassiz. In 1834, he visited Lyme Regis to see Mary and her friend Elizabeth Philpot – and Elizabeth's amazing collection of fossil fish.

Between them, Mary and Elizabeth showed Louis Agassiz 34 fossils of fish he hadn't even known about before. He was amazed at their ability to recognise different species, and fit the right fossil bones together.

Louis Agassiz

Louis Agassiz later published a book about fossil fish. In it, he thanked the women for their help – but he also did something more. He named some of the fish after them. A prehistoric shark was named *Acrodus anningiae* after Mary, and a fish was named *Eugnathus philpotae* after Elizabeth. This is a way of honouring the discoverer of a species, and keeping their name alive forever.

When Mary Anning again faced poverty, William Buckland decided to do something permanent for her. He persuaded the science clubs to which he belonged to raise a large lump sum. It was used to give Mary a pension, or regular payment, in return for all her work.

The last years

Towards the end of Mary Anning's life, she had more and more famous visitors, including the great palaeontologist Richard Owen. There was even a royal visitor, King Frederick Augustus of Saxony (part of what is now Germany). He came into Anning's Fossil Depot, and left with an ichthyosaur, bought for £15.

Richard Owen was famous for his work on fossils, but also for being rude and unpleasant. He was often featured in cartoons.

A close call

When Richard Owen visited Mary Anning, she agreed to go fossil collecting with him, William Buckland and William Conybeare. The three men found it hard to keep up with Mary on the rocks and cliffs. They ended up being cut off by the tide, and had to climb up the cliffs to escape.

In 1842, Mary Anning's mother died, at the age of 78. Mary had been very close to her and they'd always lived together. Molly had also helped to run the fossil business that supported them both. Mary was used to having quite a lonely life, but without her mother it was even lonelier.

Sometime in 1845, when she was 46, Mary Anning began feeling tired and unwell. She was suffering from cancer, which couldn't be cured. For two years she was in great pain, but still went out looking for fossils. She used laudanum, a popular painkiller at the time, to help her keep working.

Mary died in 1847, shortly before her forty-eighth birthday. She was buried in the graveyard of St Michael's Church in Lyme Regis. Her brother Joseph died two years later, aged 53, and was buried next to her.

Mary Anning's grave in Lyme Regis

At the Geological Society of London, Mary's friend Henry De la Beche read out a **eulogy** for Mary. He spoke of how she had dedicated her life to fossils. And he admitted that many of the society's members wouldn't have had such wonderful fossils to work with, if it hadn't been for her.

"They sucked my brains"

Did Mary Anning mind that men had often taken credit for her discoveries? Yes, she did. She was upset that so many of them had enjoyed successful lives as scientists, while she'd stayed poor – even though she'd often found the fossils and come up with the ideas that they'd used. In one letter to her friend Anna Pinney, she wrote:

"These men of learning have sucked my brains."

Mary Anning's legacy

Mary Anning was a great fossil finder and prehistoric animal expert. That was important in itself – but Mary also did something even more important. She helped to change science history.

When she first began finding fossils, they were mainly seen as curiosities, or old, magical stones. Her amazing discoveries helped other scientists realise there was much more to them than that. They helped to develop the new fields of geology and palaeontology, which were only just beginning.

An actor playing Mary Anning talks to visitors at London's Natural History Museum.

Thanks to fossils like the ones Anning uncovered, people saw that creatures long ago were different to those alive now. This meant that living things must have changed over a long time. These ideas led to huge changes in science, such as the **theory of evolution** in the 1800s, and the discovery of **DNA** in the 1900s.

Fossil hunters and palaeontologists are still at work today all around the world, unearthing more and more new and amazing discoveries. They are still discovering new fossils at Lyme Regis too.

Glossary

adored companion a much-loved friend

apprenticeship a way of training to do a job

belemnites prehistoric animals similar to a squid

burnished rubbed and polished until shiny

clergyman a male religious leader such as a vicar or priest

curiosities interesting or unusual items

cuttlefish a sea creature related to squid and octopuses

debate a discussion in which people present different views

DNA short for "deoxyribonucleic acid" – a chemical in living cells that controls how they live and grow

eccentric slightly strange, unusual or odd

enriched made better or more interesting

errands short journeys or tasks

eulogy speech in praise of someone who has just died

extinct no longer existing

genuine true, honest or the real thing

geology the science of rocks and the earth's history

hoax a trick, or a fake item presented as something real

imprints shapes in a surface made by something pressing on it

Jurassic a prehistoric time period, 200 to 145 million years ago

limestone a common type of rock which often contains fossils

minerals pure, natural substances that are the same all the way through and not a mixture

prehistoric from the time before history began to be written down

proceeds money made from selling something

sac a pouch or bag inside an animal

scientific papers pieces of writing about science topics

sepia a brownish ink made using cuttlefish ink

shale a type of rock that easily splits into layers

souvenirs things that remind you of a place, person or event

species the scientific name for a particular type of living thing

specimen an individual fossil, animal, piece of rock or other item, used in scientific study or as an example

theory of evolution theory of how species of living things gradually change over time

trade buying and selling things

upholsterer someone who adds the soft coverings to furniture

Index

Digging for dinosaurs

Found   1811
Name   ichthyosaur "fish-lizard"
Size   5 metres
Description   similar to today's dolphins and sharks

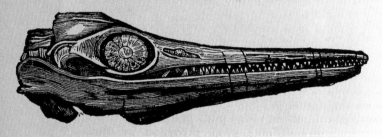

Found   1823
Name   plesiosaur "near-lizard"
Size   2.5 metres
Description   a fish-eating sea reptile

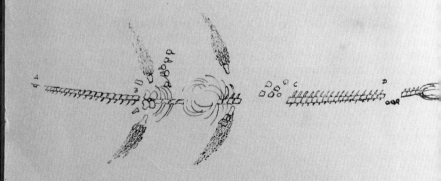

Found   1828
Name   pterosaur "winged-lizard"
Size   1.2 metres long
Description a flying or gliding reptile, related
             to dinosaurs

             the first pterosaur found in Britain

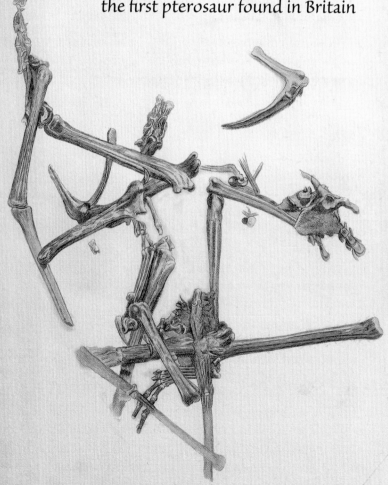

Ideas for reading

Written by Clare Dowdall, PhD
Lecturer and Primary Literacy Consultant

Reading objectives:
- discuss understanding and explore the meaning of words in context
- summarise the main ideas drawn from more than one paragraph, identifying key details that support the main ideas
- explain and discuss their understanding of what they have read, including through formal presentations and debates, maintaining a focus on the topic and using notes where necessary

Spoken language objectives:
- consider and evaluate different viewpoints, attending to and building on the contributions of others

Curriculum links: History – British history beyond 1066

Resources: ICT, art materials for drawing fossils (charcoal, paper, pencils etc), fossils if available

Build a context for reading
- Ask children to share any knowledge about fossils (what they are; where they are found; how they are made; what they are used for).
- Explain that you will be reading about a famous fossil hunter from the 19th century. Ask children to imagine what a fossil hunter's life was like.
- Look at the covers and read the blurb. Ask children if they are surprised to find that the famous fossil hunter was a woman, and if so, why.

Understand and apply reading strategies
- Look at the contents and establish that this is a type of biographical account. Help children to read any unfamiliar words, e.g. ichthyosaur.
- Discuss what the metaphors "bright spark" and "breadwinner" might suggest in relation to Mary Anning.